HAND–UP

ASSEMBLIES FOR JUNIORS

Tony Castle

**kevin
mayhew**

First published in 2002 by
KEVIN MAYHEW LTD
Buxhall, Stowmarket, Suffolk IP14 3BW
Email: info@kevinmayhewltd.com

9 8 7 6 5 4 3 2 1 0

ISBN 1 84003 993 0
Catalogue No 1500554

Cover design by Angela Selfe
Edited by Lesley Butland
Illustrations by Thomas Castle
Typesetting by Richard Weaver
Printed in Great Britain

Contents

Acknowledgements _____

The publishers wish to express their gratitude to the following for permission to include copyright material in this book:

Material from reports by CAFOD (Catholic Agency for Overseas Development) is © CAFOD, Romero Close, Stockwell Road, London SW9 9TY.

Extracts from *The Bangladesh Observer, The [Bangladesh] Independent, The [Bangladesh] Daily Star* are all © copyright of the respective newspapers.

The *Human Development Report 1999* by United Nations Development Programme, is copyright © 1999 by the United Nations Development Report Programme. Used by permission of Oxford University Press, Inc.

Anne Leahy – *75-25: Development in an Increasingly Unequal World,* published by the Development Education Centre, Birmingham, in association with CAFOD and SCIAF and Dochas of Ireland, 1996.

The extracts on *Violence against women in the churches,* and *Trafficking in women,* are taken from one of several leaflets on violence against women produced by and © copyright of the Women's Co-ordinating Group for Churches Together in England. Leaflets available from 27 Tavistock Square, London WC1H 9HH.

The article on *The Adivasis of India* is © Minority Rights Group International, 379 Brixton Road, London, SW9 7DE.

The report from *Hotline Bangladesh* is © copyright Hotline Bangladesh, GOP Box 5, Dhaka 1000, Bangladesh, and is used by permission.

The quotes from *The Tablet* are © copyright The Tablet, the international Catholic weekly, and are used by permission.

The quote from Anita Roddick in *The Big Issue* is © copyright The Big Issue, October 2001, and is used by kind permission of The Big Issue and Anita Roddick, OBE.

The quote from the *United Nations Covenant on Civil and Political Rights 1966* is © copyright the Office of the High Commissioner for Human Rights, Geneva, Switzerland.

The quote from the *Universal Islamic Declaration of Human Rights 1981* is published by and © copyright the Islamic Council, 16 Grosvenor Crescent, London SW1.

Every effort has been made to trace the owners of copyright material and we hope that no copyright has been infringed. Pardon is sought and apology made if the contrary be the case, and a correction will be made in any reprint of this book.

SECTION A

Assemblies

Introduction to Assemblies ___

Hand-up, not handout

When you are innocently out shopping, walking down the street, and you pass, or are accosted by a beggar, you are faced with an uncomfortable choice. No decent person likes to see another human being in some sort of need, 'on the street'; no Christian likes to think of him- or herself as someone who has 'passed by on the other side'. The hand outstretched seeks a response. But, and the sight of the beggar brings a 'but' into play, the question we ask ourselves is, 'Am I really helping this person by giving him/her money on the street'? We suspect that the money will be used to feed a drink or drugs problem.

This collection of assemblies is a companion to *Meeting Special People* (Kevin Mayhew, 2002), the secondary version. Both are based upon the diary I kept while visiting development projects in Bangladesh in October 2000, a trip that was funded by the Millennium Commission. (The diary was published separately as *Silent Revolution* (Kevin Mayhew, 2001).) The intention of this book is to provide the busy teacher with material to conduct the occasional assembly upon the very real problems of the ordinary people of the developing nations.

In Bangladesh we came face to face with beggars but, surprisingly, no more than you meet on British city streets. Although crushingly poor by our standards, most of the lovely, gentle people we met had too much self-respect and dignity to beg or harp upon the obvious differences between their visitors and themselves. It was very humbling to step out of a people carrier (hired to take us out to rural areas), in fashionable western clothes, clutching expensive cameras, wearing good-quality wristwatches, and stand and talk to people who had lost everything, house and home, pots and pans, livestock and all personal possessions in recent flooding. Not one of those asked us for money. They hoped that the aid agency that we were with would help them, once the flood waters receded, with the materials needed for them to go back to their piece of vacant, muddy land, and rebuild their home. They were not looking for a handout, but a hand-up.

We also learnt, to our horror, of the trafficking in women and children. Bangladesh has its share of ruthless criminals, some of whom make a lot of money from kidnapping women and children and transporting them across the border into India. There the women are sold into prostitution and the children are deliberately maimed and trained to beg on the streets for their owners. This last piece of information figured in our group discussions about giving, or not giving, to beggars. Our group of four teachers was unanimous in our belief that the answer was to give every assistance to those who were seeking a hand-up, and not to support those who were looking for a free handout.

All of these assemblies are 'proactive' in the sense that the children are not expected to be passive recipients at the assembly. Each act of collective worship begins with an engaging exchange or a challenging role play. The material can be used just as it is or merely as a prompt or springboard for a more individualised act of worship. Every school has its own favourite repertoire of songs and so none are proposed. There should be the inclusion of Scripture when and where possible, and a suggestion is provided.

At the top right-hand corner of each assembly there is a simple line drawing. It is not there just to decorate the page. It can be enlarged on a photocopier, then printed on an over-head transparency. This can be shown as an illustrative back-ground to the assembly – something to help the children to focus upon the theme of the collective act of worship.

Assembly 1
Hand-up

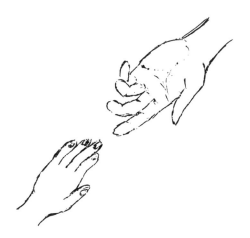

Preparations

A couple of travel brochures from a local travel agent.

Presenter

(*Standing before the group and flicking through one of the travel brochures.*) I am just looking for a really sunny, relaxing place to go for my next summer holiday. I've been to Spain and to Greece. Has anyone any ideas for me? Could you recommend a sunny place that you have been to? (*Respond to any ideas.*)

Why do people never go to Bangladesh for a holiday – unless, of course, they originally come from that country? The answer is that some countries are very poor and they do not have the holiday facilities, like comfortable hotels, that we like to have on holiday.

You have offered me some help in finding a holiday. Why do people from poor countries, like Bangladesh, never go on holiday?

They are too poor and need our help to come out of poverty.

Some teachers went to Bangladesh and it got them thinking. Let us listen to their story.

Reading

We stopped, in our car, at the traffic lights. Immediately, two beggars approached the vehicle – one on either side. On my side of the car a young woman holding a young baby on her arm was pleading for money with her hand outstretched.

On the other side it was a tall young man, dressed in rags, with just a stump for a right arm; he was begging with an out-stretched left hand. Both beggars pleaded and begged. The young mother tapped on the window only inches from my face – and I felt terrible! Christ's words, 'what you do for the least person, you do for me' came to mind, but we had been told not to give to beggars.

My friend, Stephen, sitting next to me, opened the window, and gave her a handful of sweets; but she didn't want them. We were only saved from her pleading voice by the traffic moving on from the lights.

Presenter
Why were the people in the car told not to give to beggars? (*Accept suggestions.*)

Listen now to how the teacher, who wrote the diary, finishes the story.

Reading
When we returned to the hostel where we were staying, we had a discussion about the beggars. We talked about women and children being forced to beg by other people, who then took the money from them. We spoke of the dignity that poor people have and how that should be respected. We talked about being partners with the poor – standing beside them, rather than looking down on them. We agreed that we need to look for ways to give people a hand-up, rather than a handout.

Prayer
Dear loving Father,
we believe that you care for everyone:
people with money and people without money,
people with homes and people without homes,
people with jobs and people without jobs.
May we, who live in a country
where most people have money, homes and jobs,
really try to give a hand-up to the people
who are struggling to live a happier life. Amen.

Alternatives
Scripture reading

'Has not God chosen those who are poor?' (James 2:1-5)

or

'Taking him by the hand, Peter helped him up' (Acts 3:1-8).

Assembly 2
Bike hands

Preparations

One bicycle bell. OHT of above drawing of rickshaw.

Presenter

(Ringing the bicycle bell.) Who has a bicycle bell like this one? Why does a cyclist use a bell like this one? *(Ring it again.)*

Which of you has a bicycle bell like this one? In Bangladesh this is the sound that you hear from very early in the morning, until late at night. It comes from the hundreds and hundreds of bicycle rickshaws on the streets of every city and town. The roads are crammed with them, some lorries and a few battered buses; there are very few cars.

Rickshaws are like very cheap taxis; they get people from place to place in the town. Listen now to the reading.

Reading

Delwar is a rickshaw puller, or cyclist. He has a wife and two daughters aged 6 and 8. The family came to live in the busy city a year ago, to find work, because Delwar and his wife could not earn enough money to feed the family, living in the countryside.

Delwar told us that it costs him 40 taka a day to hire the rickshaw from a big company. (That is about 60p.) He gets as many passengers as he can and, on a good day, will earn 120 taka. So he takes home to his family 80 taka; that means that he earns, in our currency, just about £1.20 a day!

Presenter

Imagine that. All the money that your family has for food and clothes and household expenses, is £1.20 a day!

Pretend for a moment that you are Delwar. How would you feel if you only brought home enough money for one meal each a day? Would you feel that is fair? Remember that the whole family is living in one room; there is no television, computer or music centre. They have none of the things that make our lives comfortable.

How can we help real people like Delwar? Yes, of course we can give generously when we have the opportunity to support one of the aid agencies, but Delwar knows we cannot help him with money. But we can be aware of how life is in the developing countries; how hard people work and how unfair things are for them. We can, and must, also pray for them.

Prayer

We live such comfortable lives, Lord,
that we forget how hard life is
for millions of our brothers and sisters in other lands.
Today we pray for all the people like Delwar,
who work so hard and get so little
to feed and support their families.
Help us to not to forget them,
and help other people
to come to know and understand their problems. Amen.

Alternatives

Scripture reading

'Stretch out your hand to the poor man' (Ecclesiasticus 7:32-36).

Assembly 3
Bound hands

Preparations A length of rope.

Presenter Who can tell me what this is? No, it is not thick string! It's a length of rope. If we are talking about hands again in this assembly and we include in our thinking some bad people, what connection might there be between 'hands' and 'rope'. (*After correct answer the OHT of the bound hands may, if possible, be shown.*)

We now have a true story, from Bangladesh, of bound hands.

Reading One sunny morning, in a remote country village of Bangladesh, Raney discovered that she had no salt left for cooking. As a working mother, Raney had no time to leave her house and go shopping at the local market. She decided to send her eldest daughter, Rosina, who was 12, to go and buy a half-kilo of salt and two kilos of rice.

Rosina complained about going but, after a few minutes, left to make the five-minute walk to the market place. Singing quietly to herself she strolled down the narrow path which, after a short distance, joined the wider earthen path to the village centre. As Rosina turned into the main path, an elegantly dressed woman, in a pale blue sari, stopped her and asked her where she was going. It was quiet and no one else seemed to be around. Rosina had never seen the woman before, but she seemed friendly and she was holding a small bunch of flowers. The woman then asked Rosina if she would like to smell her beautiful flowers. Rosina leant forward to smell them; immediately she felt dizzy and then collapsed on the path. Rosina did not see them, because she was out cold, lying on the ground, but at this point two men stepped out from the undergrowth where they had been hiding.

When Rosina came round she found that her arms and legs were bound and there was a dirty rag over her mouth. She was confused and did not know where she was; it seemed to be a rough shed. To her surprise there were five other children lying close to her in the shed. Then she heard voices; a woman's voice and a man's voice. The woman asked, 'When are you moving them out?' The man replied, 'We'll get a couple more and then we'll get the van round to collect them.' Rosina knew immediately what was happening. They had to get out of that hut and fast. She had heard of children being kidnapped and taken across the border into India; there they were sold to be beggars and slaves. She and the others had to get out! As she was trying to signal with her eyes to one of the other children, she noticed that one young boy was rubbing his bound wrists against a wooden post that supported the ceiling. In a few minutes he got himself free and then started untying the others. Rosina was so relieved to get her arms and legs free and warned everyone to stay silent as they looked for a way out. The walls of the hut were very flimsy, made from woven banana leaves. Very soon they had found a small hole, which they made bigger, and were crawling out, one after the other.

It took Rosina three hours to walk from the town of Khulna, where she had been held. It was late in the evening when she finally stumbled into her home and the arms of her frightened mother.

Presenter

It is a terrible truth that about 100 children and women are kidnapped and taken from their homes and families every month. They are never seen again! Isn't that a dreadful thought?

We must thank God that we live in a safe, secure country where it is hard to imagine that happening to us, or to our families or friends. We need to pray for boys and girls, in far-away countries, like Bangladesh, where it does happen. We must also pray that powerful people, like governments and the United Nations, will work hard to stop it.

Prayer

Dear loving Father,
we find it hard to believe
that such terrible things can happen to women and children.
We would be so unhappy
if anything dreadful happened to the people we love.
Father, you love those people;
please protect them from harm.
May they find happiness; may they find freedom. Amen.

Alternatives

Scripture

'My ways are not your ways' (Isaiah 55:7-9).

(Word of caution: if this assembly is used, it must be made very clear, more than once, that the events described happen far away, in a poor country in Asia. They do not happen, as such, here.)

14

Assembly 4
Child's hands

Presenter

(Use OHP to show the child's drawing. Indicating the drawing.) What is it? It's not very special, is it?

Who do you think drew it? Who thinks they could draw a better picture of a chicken? And so you should, because you have been coming to school regularly for a few years now.

You have three, perhaps four, meals a day.

You have a nice cosy bed and perhaps your own bedroom.

You are beginning to think, 'What's all that to do with the drawing?'

Well, the girl who drew this picture of a chicken was 8 years of age and she lives in Bangladesh. Her name is Shahidha.

Let's listen to a reading about her.

Reading

We then visited the slum school. Three sessions take place every evening after normal school time, at the nearby Notre Dame High School. Four hundred children from the streets attend each session. The teachers are senior students from the High School, who do not get paid for taking the evening classes for the street children.

We walked into the very big, but sparse and poorly furnished, classrooms and spoke to the children, who got very excited by our visit. I tried, not very successfully, to speak to 8-year-old Shahidha, who was from the slums. She was very shy, but I learnt that she cannot go to school during the day, because her family are too poor. She has to work cleaning people's houses; otherwise there will not be enough food to feed the family. She comes to school most evenings from 7.30 to 9pm, because she wants to learn to read and write. I looked at her exercise book where she had drawn a chicken. I wrote my name in pencil beside hers, on the page. As we left the class-rooms the street children came out of class and excitedly mobbed us.

Presenter

(If time permits.) Here is another true story of a street boy; this time from Ghana, one of the countries of Africa.

Reading

Kwame is a 14-year-old shoeshine boy. He sleeps each night at the lorry park in the city of Accra, under one of the lorries for shelter. He wakes as soon as it gets light and buys some water from the local water lorry to wash with. By 6.30am Kwame will be looking for the women who sell food on the streets. If he has kept enough money from the day before he will buy some rice water or porridge and a piece of bread for his breakfast. Then he will join the crowds heading for the city centre with his precious bowl of shoeshining materials under his arm. He has his own patch of pavement but may have to fight another boy to drive him off, to protect his area.

Kwame will be there all day, through the terrible humid heat of the day. If he has a good day he may earn the equivalent of £1; if he has a bad day he will be hungry. He finishes as it gets dark and heads back to the lorry park. Chances are that he will be fast asleep by 10 o'clock, having first paid for water to drink, wash with and to use a toilet. He will also have to pay a watchman to guard his shoeshine box while he is asleep under a lorry.

Prayer

Almighty Father,
it must be terrible to have no proper home;
to live on the streets, under lorries or in big cardboard boxes.
Yet many thousands of children, who are our age,
do live like that.
What can we ask you, Lord?
Can you help us to be really grateful for our own homes?
Can you send children, like Shahidha and Kwame,
adults who will help them?
Can you get governments to take some real action?
Can you help us to be more generous when we are asked
to support agencies that help street children?
Father, may we have a loving concern and do what we can.
Amen.

Alternatives

Scripture reading

'Let the little children come to me' (Matthew 19:14-15).

Assembly 5
Clenched hands

Presenter

I want you all to clench your fists, like this. It looks like a hammer, doesn't it? It looks quite fierce, when everyone has clenched fists.

What would you do with a hand like this? Yes, it reminds us of fighting and violence. Please unclench your hands.

What is bullying? Yes, it is when one person, or a small group of people, get picked on. It is very wrong that they get picked on, but sometimes we hear about that sort of thing happening.

Can you give me some examples of the sort of people who might (not in this school, we hope) get picked on? (*Sensitive handling required.*)

In our country and around the world, there are groups of people who get picked on. For example, gypsies or refugees. Can you think of any other small groups who get picked on.

Here are a few examples:

- In Australia, the Aborigines might get picked on.
- In some parts of London, Asian people might get picked on.
- In Liverpool, a Manchester United supporter might get picked on.

There are lots of examples.

But stop . . . and reflect.

Do you think that Jesus would ever pick on anyone?

Presenter

In Bangladesh there are the Garo people who get picked on by the majority of the population. They live in the north of the country, in villages in the big forest there. Hundreds of years ago these tribal people came from Nepal and settled in Bangladesh. They are smaller than the local Bangla people and they have round faces. They are bullied by some of the local landowners and their land is stolen from them.

One priest, Father Homerich, speaks up for them.

Reading

I've been living in the forest with the Garo people for many years. I am helping them with legal advice and lawyers when they are robbed of their land. Because they are the minority they get picked on by the majority Bangla community.

At the moment I am involved with several hundred legal cases. Most of them are to do with forest rights and rights to wood and land. These belong to Garo people by tradition; unfortunately their rights are not written down.

Presenter

There are many Christian heroes, like that priest, around the world, who speak up for the poor when they get picked on. They and the people they are defending need our prayers.

Prayer

Dear God,
it is terrible to be picked on and bullied.
Your Son, Jesus, was picked on, tortured and killed;
so you, loving God, know all about your people
who are picked on; and those who are bullied.
Every year hundreds of people die for being Christians.
Every year hundreds of people are tortured
and held in prison, because of their beliefs.
We pray for anyone, and everyone,
who at this moment, as we pray now to you,
is being picked on, hurt and bullied. Amen.

Alternatives

Scripture

'Bless those who persecute you' (Romans 12:14-19).

Assembly 6
Community hands

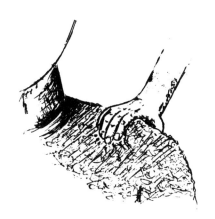

With this assembly the activity can precede the reading or it can follow the reading according to the judgement of the presenter.

Presenter

We are going to have a short activity but we are going to do it in perfect silence; there is no need to whisper or giggle.

I would like you all to stand and, unless you are in the front row, you are standing one behind the other, with another pupil on each side of you. Now, please place your left hand on the shoulder of the person in front of you . . . place your right hand on the shoulder of the person to your right.

Electricity is a hidden power that runs along wires and cables. It gives energy and lights up people's lives.

Love is a hidden power that runs between people. It gives energy and lights up people's lives.

Think now of love flowing from you into the person in front of you and to the person alongside you. Imagine how it can give energy to both those persons . . . and to you.

Without moving, think in your head, a loving prayer for the people you are touching . . . simple like 'Dear God, look after these two persons today.'
We love God by loving one another. Hands down. Please sit down.

The reading you are going to hear now is set in Bangladesh, which is a very poor country, where some people have decided to work together in groups in order to support one another. The reading is from a diary kept during a visit by a teacher from England.

Reading

We got out of the people carrier and walked down an earthen path into a small community area of mud houses. There were 24 women in bright coloured saris waiting patiently for us. They were sitting cross-legged on ground in a rough square. We took off our sandals and sat down with them.

They introduced themselves and then we did the same. We asked them questions about their lives and there was lots of laughter. Their simple innocent questions to us revealed that they had not the slightest idea what life in England is like. 'Are your houses like ours, made of mud?' 'Is life a struggle for you, like it is for us?'

The group met once every two weeks to organise their savings and also for education about sanitation and hygiene. We had to move on but we could happily have stayed there much longer talking to these confident, cheerful, but very poor, struggling women.

Prayer

God, our loving Father,
you gave us Jesus,
who taught us to love and respect one another.
Help us never to forget
that we are all members of your family;
we need to help and support one another,
in love, at all times.
May our hands be always used in friendship and love,
to the glory of your name. Amen.

Alternatives

Scripture reading

'All the believers were together' (Acts 2:42-47).

Assembly 7
Dirty hands

Presenter

Please show your hands to the boy or girl on your right.

Now, own up. Who has the dirtest hands here today?

If your hands were dirty and I said, 'You must clean them', what would you do? Does it sound like a silly question?

You would say, 'I'll go to the toilets and wash them.'

But, what if we had no toilets, or we had no taps and basins in the school where you could wash your hands, what would you do then?

Listen now to our reader.

Reader

In most villages and towns in Bangladesh, the houses and schools have no water taps. If they are very lucky, they have a water pump nearby. But most people wash in the local pond or stream.

Presenter

Sounds strange to us, doesn't it? I want you now to think of your home. Close your eyes and imagine your house. How many taps, for hot and cold water, do you have? Upstairs in the bathroom, include the kitchen and, perhaps, the utility room.

Let's see, in my home we have x number of taps. Does anyone have more than that? (*Take suggested numbers from hands raised.*)

Aren't we very lucky to live in a wealthy country where we have so much water coming into our houses. In Bangladesh, we heard, most people share a water pump in the street or village square.

Reading

Outside the small house, in a tiny square, stood a pump. It was a rower pump, with a handle that you had to pull towards you for the water to come out of the pipe. I stepped across to have a go; I pulled the handle and out came the water; pushed the handle in and nothing happened. I pulled the handle towards me again, and out came the water. The young interpreter stepped up to me and asked, 'Do you have pumps like that in your villages and streets?' 'No,' I replied.

He looked worried and concerned. 'You don't have pumps?' 'No,' I said, 'every house has a tap.' He repeated what I had said. 'Every house has a tap! That is wonderful.' He repeated it again as a question, '*Every* house has a tap?' 'Yes,' I said, 'we are very fortunate.' I did not tell him that every house has many taps, a bath and perhaps a shower; he was amazed enough about one tap!

Prayer

Almighty God,
thank you for water.
It sounds strange to say, 'thank you' for water,
because it's always there; we never even think about it.
But without water we would die;
just like air,
we need it all day, every day.
Please help us to appreciate water,
and be always grateful for it.
May all those people in the world
who do not have a safe, clean supply of water, get one soon.
Amen.

Alternatives

Scripture

'Will you give me a drink?' (John 4:4-14).

Assembly 8
Distressed hands

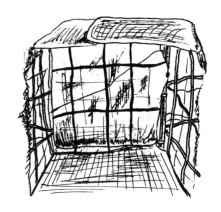

Preparations

Either use the picture and make an overhead transparency to show, or build a simple shelter before the assembly. It must be in full view. The 'shelter' is extremely simple and will take a couple of minutes to construct. Find two tables of equal length and width, approximately 1½-2 m long. Stand them on their ends, so that the table tops are vertical, facing out, with the four legs of each table facing one another; four form the floor of the shelter and four the roof. Drape a short old curtain or sheet over the top four legs.

Presenter

Imagine that you are very upset. What might you do with your hands? Yes, wipe away tears or cover your face with your hands. It's a gesture that says, 'I want to cut myself off from other people; leave me alone, I want to be left alone in my distress.'

(Indicating either the projected OHT picture or the constructed shelter.) What do you think this is? Yes, it is a tiny shack or shelter. Look at it as we listen to the reading.

Reading

Further up the road we witnessed flood destruction and many, many more displaced people – half a million had lost their homes. We stopped at a little encampment and a small crowd gathered; we were immediately besieged by curious adults and children as we wandered into it.

We interviewed a young mother, Puspa, who was sitting on a rush mat in a shelter which was a cube in shape, 2 m by 2 m by 2 m, with no possessions to be seen. Snuggled up to her was Madori, her two-and-a-half-year-old daughter. Puspa told us how, four weeks before, the waters had come pouring into her home at 3 o'clock in the morning.

They were taken completely by surprise. The waters were so strong and deep that they washed down the walls of the house. They had run for their lives. We asked Puspa how long she might have to live with her family of three children in this tiny shack; she said, 'Perhaps another four weeks, until the waters go down and we can go back and rebuild our home.'

Presenter When you so generously give your money to Aid agencies (*like CAFOD, Christian Aid, etc.*) you are helping people like Puspa. Now you can see why I have (*built a shack . . . shown the picture*) so that you can see and understand what people in disaster areas have to do to cope with life. Let us say a prayer for people like Puspa who lose their homes and possessions in disasters like floods, typhoons, earthquakes and so on.

Prayer Heavenly Father,
we are all your children, wherever we live in the world.
Some of us never have terrifying earthquakes or tidal waves,
or terrible flooding that washes away our homes.
We thank you for that.
Today we pray for the people
who do suffer such dreadful tragedies;
especially the poor who have no money
and rely on the help we can provide.
May we always be kind, understanding and generous. Amen.

Alternatives *Scripture reading*

'Do everything without complaining' (Philippians 2:14-18).

Assembly 9
Excluding hands

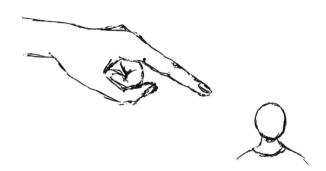

Preparations

Choose a pupil (Y) and brief her/him. Tell them, confidentially, that you are going to point at them at the beginning of the assembly, pretend to be angry and send them out; it is just a dramatic opening and no hurt is intended. Prepare seven pupils for the 'demonstration' used below.

Presenter

Today we are going to talk about 'exclusion'. In schools, someone who is 'excluded' is prevented from attending classes. There are millions of people in the world who are excluded from mixing with others and doing what other people do. For example . . . *(Stop abruptly, point at 'prepared' pupil)* . . . what do you think you are doing . . . that's no way to behave . . . get out! Now! *(Pupil leaves the area.)* As I was saying, there are millions of people in the world who are excluded. For example, in some societies women are not allowed to take part in everyday life; they are not allowed to sit with the men; not allowed to vote; not allowed to say what they think. They are excluded.

Presentation

The seven pupils are now invited out to the front. Six stand in a circle, facing one another, their hands, palms open, extended behind them. The seventh one (X) wanders round the outside of the circle, excluded.

Presenter

How do you think X feels, excluded from the group? Would you like to be excluded? *(Group remains still as the 'excluded' pupil returns.)* How do think Y felt to be excluded from what we are doing?

Let's ask them how they felt about being excluded.

In St John's Gospel we read of a woman who has been excluded from her community. She is a Samaritan, to whom Jesus should not, as a good Jew, have been talking, because the Jews of that time excluded the Samaritans.

Reading
Jesus once had to cross Samaria, and he came, about midday, to Jacob's Well, outside the Samaritan town of Sychar. His friends went off into the town to buy some food. The long walk had tired Jesus and he sat down, just as he was, near the well. A Samaritan woman came along to draw water.

'Could you please give me a drink?' he asked.

'Indeed!' she said. 'You're a Jew – and you are asking me, a Samaritan woman, to give you a drink?'

'If you only understood the Jewish religion', said Jesus, 'and who it was who is asking you for a drink, you would have asked him for a drink . . . not well water, but living water.'

His friends came back from the town. They were amazed to find him talking with a woman. They were too amazed even to ask him if he wanted anything to eat, let alone why he was talking with her.

The woman left her pitcher by the well and went off back to the town.   *The Alan Dale Bible,* version of St John, chapter 4.*

Presenter
Did you notice, Jesus did not exclude the Samaritan woman; he was quite prepared to shock his friends, who thought he should exclude her. So the lesson for us is clear; even if our friends are unkind and exclude someone, we should never do that. Always do the kind thing.

Prayer
Dear Jesus,
you loved everyone
and never excluded anyone because they were different.
You were not supposed to speak to a woman, but you did.
You were not supposed to speak to a foreigner, but you did.
Your loving kindness is a great example to us.
May we never exclude people, never be unkind. Amen.

Alternatives
Scripture

'Be kind and compassionate to one another' (Ephesians 4:29-32).

---

* *The Alan Dale Bible,* Kevin Mayhew, 2002.

Assembly 10
Greeting hands

Preparations

(If the time of the year (and place) permits.) A small bouquet of wild flowers or simple flowers (daffodils?) from the garden.

Presenter

(Holding bunch of flowers.) When do you think I might receive a bunch of flowers like this one? *(Accept reasonable suggestions.)* When might you buy a bunch of flowers for someone? *(Accept reasonable suggestions.)*

In some cultures, for example among the Hindu people who live in Bangladesh, flowers can be used to welcome strangers.

Reading

We were going to visit a school for very poor children, way out in the beautiful countryside. In the bright sunshine the farm workers were cutting and bringing in the rice harvest. We left the reasonably smooth road to bump and bounce along a very rough track for about 20 minutes and then we arrived at the school. It was like a long farm shed with a corrugated iron roof. But what a welcome! About 60 very poorly dressed children – infants and juniors – were lined up in two long lines, with the youngest in the front. Those in the front carried posies of flowers. A little girl stepped forward and said, in English that she had obviously learnt by heart and practised many times, 'We are poor and can offer you nothing but our flowers, our song and our love.' The whole group sang a beautiful song in Bengali while girls stepped forward and gave each of us a lovely bunch of flowers. It was such a wonderful greeting that I nearly cried.

Presenter

How do we greet visitors when they come to our school? Could we do more to make them welcome? If poor children can do that, can we not be more welcoming at school and at home?

Prayer

Dear Lord,
you have said that when we welcome people,
we welcome you;
if we are discourteous to people,
we are discourteous to you.
May we always show respect to everyone
for you love them and expect us to do the same. Amen.

Alternatives

Scripture reading

'When did we see you a stranger?' (Matthew 25:31-46).

Assembly 11
Praying hands

Preparations

Two volunteers are needed to practise and enact the 'blessing' spoken of below.

Presenter

(Confidently standing before the assembled group with arms up and outstretched.) Can anyone tell me, from this posture, what they think this assembly is about? No, I am not pretending to be a scarecrow – thank you very much!

The answer is *(lowering the arms)* prayer. That posture of mine was the way Christians used to pray hundreds of years ago. They stood and held their arms up, like that, when they prayed. Quite a number of very old wall paintings, in the Roman cemeteries, called catacombs, show the first Christians praying in that way.

Would anyone, now, like to stand and show me what we do with our hands nowadays? *(Hands together in traditional fashion.)*

Can you pray without doing this with your hands? Yes, of course you can. So why do we do it? A mark of respect is the answer. I wonder where Christians got the idea from?

Reading

Wherever we went in Bangladesh we received a warm welcome. Most people would stop, put both their hands together on their chests and give a little bow of the head, with a smile. The country people in the villages became quite confused when we tried to shake hands. That's not part of their culture and they do not have physical contact like that.

Presenter

Perhaps our idea of how to address God came originally from the East. After all, that's where the Christian faith started. Here is another short reading.

Reading

We had made a visit to a riverside village and were just about to leave. Our hosts, who had entertained us to a lovely meal of rice and fish, came to the river bank to see us off on the rough and noisy engine boat. They put their hands together and bowed their heads; however, Ahmed, an elderly gentleman, did something extra. Having joined his hands, he looked straight at me and placed his right hand, palm open on his breast. He bowed. I smiled and repeated his action back to him; Ahmed gave a broad smile, turned and left the group.

The interpreter said to me, 'Do you know what you have done?' With great anxiety, because I suspected that I had done something wrong, I said, 'No, what I have done?' 'You have promised to pray for him. That gesture says, "I will pray for you".' I was very relieved and said, 'We will pray for one another; he a Moslem and I a Christian.'

Presenter

So this is what Ahmed did *(matching actions to words):* two hands together – disengage right hand, and place, with palm open, on to left of the chest.

Now we watch it done by two volunteers. *(These now come out and demonstrate.)*

Prayer

Almighty Father,
you are the God who loves and created all people,
whatever their religion;
you are not just the God of Christian people.
You know all, you love all,
and receive praise and prayer from everyone
who sincerely seeks and turns to you.
May we always respect people
who have a different religion from us.
May we respect their culture and their ways,
and be ready to learn new and good things from them. Amen.

Alternatives

Scripture reading

'Two men went to the Temple to pray' (Luke 18:10-14).

Assembly 12
Sewing hands

Preparations

Have a shirt or blouse to hold up at the beginning.

Presenter

Have a look at the cuffs on your shirts or blouses *(adapt to conditions)*. What do you see? What holds the shirt together? Yes, cotton thread.

How did it get there? Yes it could be done by hand – a person sewing without a machine or, much more likely, it was done by a fast sewing machine.

Does anyone know where in the world – in which countries – most of our clothes are made? Yes, China, Thailand, Korea, Bangladesh. Has anyone got a brother or sister of 14? Are they at school? In those countries that you told me about, most boys and girls of 14 are not at school. They are at work. They are making clothes.

Let's hear about where these young workers live.

Reading

We were taken to meet the garment workers who make the clothes for our High Street shops, like Gap. The car dropped us off in a congested street and we walked down some filthy lanes, with thin, staring folk working on or beside the pavement; or just sitting. Then we went along a very narrow bamboo walkway, above an evil-looking, smelly rubbish tip full of rotting rubbish. Next, we clambered down a narrow passageway, passing 'rooms' that were people's homes. We stepped up into one of these rooms, which was about the size of the average bedroom back home in Britain. Four people lived in this home. We, the visitors, sat on a large raised platform, which must have been the sleeping area. People – most were teenage girls – from outside crowded in to see us and talk to us.

Presenter

If you wondered what a slum is, you have just heard about one. It is where people who are poor are forced to live because they do not have enough money to live anywhere better. Slums often have no proper water supply or electricity;

although the one you have just heard about did have both of those things.

Now let us hear about Asma, a 14-year-old girl who lives in the home we have just heard about.

Reading

We were introduced to Asma, who told us that she was 14 years old. She said that she did not mind us asking her some questions. We asked if this was her home; she said that she lived in this room with her aunt and uncle and a female cousin.

Her parents lived in the north and they had sent her to the city when she was 11 to live with her aunt and uncle and get a job. She has been making clothes for European shops for the last three years. She works on a sewing machine and must make 60 collars for shirts every hour. She told us that she started work at 8am and usually worked every day, that is seven days a week, for £5 a week. Sometimes she has to work right into the night; then she sleeps down beside her sewing machine at work. Asma's day begins at 5am; after breakfast, washing clothes and clearing up, she has to walk three miles to the factory. She cannot take time off work if she is ill because, if she does, the job is given to someone else.

Presenter

In the future, when we go shopping with our family, we should remember who it is that makes the clothes that we buy in our High Street shops. Let us use this opportunity to think of those children and teenagers and pray for them.

Prayer

Dear, caring Father,
you have given us hands, that we may feed ourselves,
help ourselves, make things and play.
We have been thinking of your children,
who have to spend all day, every day, working in factories,
unable to help themselves and unable to play, as we do.
It is very unfair, Lord, and we ask that one day
there may be more fairness and more happiness
for the children and teenagers of the countries
that make the clothes. Amen.

Alternatives

Scripture text

'What we suffer can never be compared' (Romans 8:18, 22-24).

Assembly 13
Skilled hands

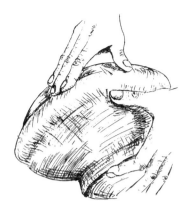

Preparations

Two flower pots from the garden are required: a brown plastic one and a clay one; both the same size if possible.

Presenter

(Showing the group the two pots; one in each hand.) I have here two brown plant pots from my garden. Can you look at them and tell me what the difference is? Yes, one is made of plastic and one is made of clay. The first was made by a machine in a factory and the second one could have been made by a potter on a potter's wheel. (Actually it was probably made on a machine; but pots like this one were once made, in this country, on a potter's wheel.)

Let's stop and reflect. Which of these two pots is cheaper to make? Why the plastic one? Yes, hundreds can be made in a few minutes on modern machines. Why would the clay or pottery one cost more?

Let's now pretend. If you were a potter and you had been making pots like these on your wheel for many years, what would you be worried about? Yes, that no one would want your pots, because they cost more. If you can't sell your pots, you will not be able to feed your family.

There is now a reading about this to listen to.

Reading

On our return journey, we made an unscheduled stop at a roadside potter's workshop. The potter's name was Dullchander and he was a big and powerfully built middle-aged man. He invited us into his open-sided workshop where, swiftly and expertly, he 'threw' a clay pot for us.

I was surprised by the huge wheel that he was using – the size of a small tractor wheel. The wheel was horizontal to the ground and he spun it by standing over it and making it revolve with the stick he had in his hand. When it was going very fast he sat down and placed the lump of clay on a little platform in the centre of the wheel. In no time at all he had shaped the pot with his very skilful hands; and it was finished.

Presenter   We use a different type of potter's wheel in this country, but the skill of the potter's hands is the same. Let us continue with our reading.

Reading   Dullchander, who had been a potter all his life, like his father and grandfather before him, told us that work for potters was declining. There had been many potters in the district when he was a boy, but now he was the last one. Plastic pots made in factories were killing his trade. There would be no future for his son. He would be forced to go into the cities to find work.

Presenter   (*Holding the plastic flower pot.*) When we go shopping we can often find cheap goods, like this flower pot, but we need to ask ourselves if buying cheap means that other people are losing their jobs, and will have no money to support themselves and their families, even though we save money. Let us pray.

Prayer   We pray, Almighty God,
for the people in developing countries
who have skills and work so hard,
but do not earn enough money
to have a happy and secure life.
May we, who enjoy a very comfortable life
and have money to spare for all kinds of extra luxuries,
remember the poor.
May we use every opportunity to help them
and show our gratitude to you, Lord,
for your generosity to us, by our generosity to them. Amen.

Alternatives   *Scripture*

'I went down to the potter's house' (Jeremiah 18:1-6).

Assembly 14
Unique hands

Preparations

A handful of variegated evergreen leaves from the garden. Give these out (keeping just one back) to the pupils who are at, or near the front.

Presenter

(Holding up the leaf to view.) I have here an evergreen leaf. It is called a variegated evergreen, because it has a pattern in yellow (or a lighter green). There are more along the front here. *(Addressing the front row.)* Please hold your leaf up for all to see. Now look more closely at your leaf . . . then compare it with the leaf on either side of you. What do you see? What have you discovered? Yes, yours is different from the others. Each leaf is unique; that means all variegated leaves are different from one another. God only creates unique leaves.

Now, I want you to hold up your right-hand thumb. Hold it right up high, so that I can see it, for the Thumb Test. So now I can see x number of thumbs. They all look the same from where I am standing. What will make every one different? Yes, your thumbprint. Yes, every thumb here is different from every other thumb in the world. Your thumb is unique. God only creates unique thumbs. That means that you, the whole of you, is unique. You are a special person. Let's listen to the reading.

Reading

I have made a remarkable discovery. We are all special! I'm special and you are special. I am unique and you are unique.

I made this discovery when I realised that every cow is different from every other cow; every dog is different from every other dog, every leaf on every tree in the world is different from every other leaf. It's exciting to realise that God only makes uniquely. He never makes two of anything exactly the same; even identical twins are different from one another.

So if I'm special, then you are special. If I am special then each of the people I see in the street is special.

Presenter
There are loving and brave people in the world who never forget how special everyone is. They risk their lives to help them.

Reading
Rosalind is a middle-aged woman who is unmarried. She has dedicated her life to speaking up for people who cannot help themselves. She is a Human Rights co-ordinator. Fearlessly she has taken up the cause of the young garment workers, the tribal peoples and anyone who is treated unfairly. She has to have a bodyguard to accompany her because she has been beaten up several times by thugs sent by the landowners or factory owners. Rosalind told us gripping stories of the people she had helped and the cases against unjust employers, factory owners and landowners.

Presenter
Remembering how special and unique everyone is, let us pray for people who are not treated fairly and who suffer violence for their beliefs in the dignity of everyone.

Prayer
Look down at your open hands as we say this prayer.

Father Creator,
I want to say thank you for my hands.
They are very special to me;
they are different from my friend's hands
and the hands of everyone here.
The whole of me is specially made by you, dear God.
I think it is wonderful that I am special and unique.
Every boy and girl, every grown-up living in the poor countries
is also special and unique, and dear to you.
Every person should be treated fairly,
should live in peace and be treated equally and fairly.
May all the people around the world who work and suffer
so that the poor may be loved and respected,
be blessed, made strong and kept safe. Amen.

Alternatives
Scripture reading

'Let us make man in our image' (Genesis 1:26-30).

Assembly 15
Begging hands

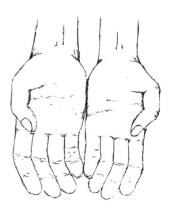

Preparations

Three pupils prepared to act the scene from Acts 3:1-10, taking the roles of Peter, John and the beggar. This can be acted with the pupils knowing their words, or role-played as the text is read.

Presenter

We are going to start with a short play from the New Testament. After the death and resurrection of Jesus, his friends try to carry on with their lives. One day, on the way to the Temple to pray, Peter and John meet someone.

Play

Acts 3:1-10.

Presenter

Did you notice that Peter and John gave the beggar something more important than money? They gave him back his health and his dignity. 'Taking him by the right hand, Peter helped the beggar up.' Peter gave the beggar a hand-up.

That is our role, offering people in need a hand-up. People who beg on the streets always have deeper problems than money for a meal. The beggar helped by Peter and John had been crippled all his life. He could not work and support himself. To restore his health was to make it possible to feed himself every day.

Reading

As our car stopped at the traffic lights, the same two beggars that we had seen each day came up to the car. There was the young woman with a child, and the young man with a stump for a right arm.

Now that I knew they were here, begging at the traffic lights, all day every day, and it was their way of life and that they could have jobs if they wanted them, I felt better about saying 'no' to them. We teachers were all convinced that it is better to give people a hand-up than a handout.

Prayer

Heavenly Father,
there are many very poor people in the world.
We believe that you have always shown a special love
and concern for them;
may we show the same love and concern.
We believe that you have blessed us
with the privilege of living in a wealthy country;
we enjoy so many good things in our lives.
May we be always grateful to you and show our gratitude
in a loving care for the poor, who are your special concern.
Amen.

Alternatives

Scripture

'Bartimaeus was sitting begging' (Mark 10:46-52).

Assembly 16
Working hands

Preparation

A length of rope and a heavy table (or similar piece of furniture) are required. A small selection of boys and girls is briefed for participation. There will need to be some experimentation, and a practice, by the group before the assembly.

Presenter

How many of you know the story, probably read to you when you were little, of the 'Enormous Turnip'? Can you tell us the outline?

Yes, first the farmer takes hold of the big turnip and pulls and nothing happens; then his wife helps, and the turnip doesn't move. Their children help and even their dog and their cat lend a paw! In the end the turnip only comes out of the ground when the mouse helps. Think about that for a moment.

Presentation

The rope has been tied round the leg of the heavy table. Now, either it can really be too heavy for the pupil to move by pulling the rope, or the pupil pretends to be unable to move the table by pulling the rope. A second pupil is called out to add her pulling power . . . then another and another. Finally the table can be dragged along only when the smallest pupil joins the end of the rope and pulls.

Presenter

Before our volunteers sit down, let me ask you to remember the 'Enormous Turnip'. What do that story and what we have just seen teach us?

Yes, when we work with our hands we are all equal; the biggest and the smallest. But, even more important, the contribution of the smallest person is valuable. It needed the mouse to pull up the turnip and we needed X to pull the table. Working together makes us strong.

That is the lesson that poor people in the developing countries, like Bangladesh, have discovered. Everyone matters and, if people work together in groups, they can start to defeat poverty.

Reading

A famous woman named Margaret Mead once said:

> Never doubt that a small group of committed people can change the world. Indeed, it is the only thing that ever has.

Presenter

Before we say our prayer, let us stop and reflect upon our own lives, here at school.

In the minute or two of silence which we are now going to have, ask yourself:

- Do we work together to make things better in our school?
- Do I respect what the smallest person in the school can do?
- Do I do my best to make things better?

Prayer

Dear God,
you did not give us hands to hang idly by our sides.
You did not give us hands just to take from others.
You gave us hands to work.
You gave us hands to help other people.
You gave us hands to develop our skills and talents.
You gave us hands to give you praise and glory.
May we always be generous in offering to lend a hand. Amen.

Alternatives

Scripture

'All the believers were together' (Acts 2:42-47).

SECTION B
Resources

Introduction to Resources

Collective worship in school should work on the stimulus-response principle. The assembly leader provides, directly or indirectly, a stimulus to elicit a prayerful response from the assembled pupils. To be effective, a stimulus cannot be long or too detailed. However, a stimulating commencement to an assembly may touch upon and raise a very important issue that should not be treated lightly. For example, to use the plight of garment workers as a stimulus is legitimate, but it is cruelly unjust to the young girls to leave it there. To use their story involves us. Having met and talked with these exploited children and young women, I know that they would, at the very least, expect us to be properly informed, to enlighten others and, where it is possible, use our power as consumers to protest.

This section is a collection of facts, and further stories and illustrations that can be used to inform teaching in the classroom. (Naturally it is not for pupil use.) Apart from a few examples I have not presumed to tell the teacher how to use the material. It seems to me that it can be used not only in the RE lesson, and in English to stimulate creative writing, but also in geography and in a study of global citizenship. The websites referred to have a mass of further information and the aid agencies – CAFOD, Christian Aid, for example – publish fact sheets and are always willing to help. All the agencies have videos that can be purchased or loaned. They will also be happy to provide speakers if requested.

Resource 1
Partners with the poor – aid agencies

Fact file:

What is poverty?

Not having the minimum income level to get the necessities of life.

'More than a lack of what is necessary for material well-being, poverty can also mean the denial of opportunities and choices most basic to human development.'

The State of Human Development, 1998

Percentage of people living below the poverty line

According to internationally accepted standards, anyone earning less than 60p (US$1) a day is living below the poverty line, i.e. does not earn enough to live on.

Europe and Central Asia	3.5%
Middle East and North Africa	4.1%
Latin America and Caribbean	23.5%
Sub-Saharan Africa	38.5%
South Asia	43.1%

In total 1.3 billion people live on less than 60p a day.

Over 80 countries have lower incomes per person today than they did ten years ago. *Human Development Report, 1999*

What is development?

- Development *is about people;*
- Development *is about people making choices;*
- Development *is about people making choices based on values;*
- Development *is about people making choices based on values about the quality of life.*

Using ICT

Try these websites:
www.eti.org.uk   Ethical Trading Initiative
www.undp.org   United Nations Development Programme

Caritas
(the word means 'love')

is the name of the aid and relief agency of the Catholic Church. In England and Wales it is called CAFOD. In the rest of the world it is known as 'Caritas'. It is found in 161 countries and, after the United Nations, it is the biggest aid agency in the world. Each 'Caritas' is independent and an arm of the local Catholic Bishops' Conference. A bishop is always the president, other members of the governing body are elected.

In Bangladesh, for example, there is a head office in Dhaka and seven regional offices (some with guest houses and conference facilities). It is dedicated to:

- integrated development
- disaster management
- human resource development.

The vision of Caritas Bangladesh is in accordance with the social teachings of the Catholic Church. Caritas is in search of a new humanism, which will enable humanity today to find itself anew by embracing higher values of life and friendship, of prayer, contemplation and compassion. Caritas professes the growth of the person from a less human to a more human state of life through integral development of the 'whole person'.

Which term?

'North–South divide', 'Developing nations' or 'Third World'?

North–South A phrase originating from the Brandt Report of 1980. It is a simple way of showing how the world is divided into rich and poor. The rich **North** includes North America, Europe, Japan, Australia, and New Zealand. The poor **South** includes most of Asia, Africa and Latin America.

However, it is not quite accurate because of Australia and New Zealand.

Third World The phrase 'Third World' originated in France in the 1950s and was a politically motivated term. There was the first world of capitalism, the second world of communism and the third world of non-aligned (and so, poor) countries.

With the fall of communism there is no second world. Many people – including the poor themselves – still prefer this term. Its original intent is still relevant, for it draws attention to the disparity in the distribution and use of world power.

Developing countries (nations) This is currently the phrase most in use. It can however, give false impressions. It implies that the western world is already developed (in what sense?) and the poorer world is now developing in the same direction. (Is this entirely desirable?) It is also incorrect because the world's poor have increased in number while the gap between rich and poor continues to widen.

Resource 2
Movement into the cities – rickshaw pullers

Delwar, who featured in the reading, moved into the city of Dhaka to find work. He had been a farm worker but there was not enough work for him to support his wife and two daughters, so he moved into the city.

Fact file

'Urbanisation' is the name given to the movement of people from the countryside (the rural setting) into the towns and cities. It has been taking place for hundreds of years. Two hundred years ago it was a major problem in Great Britain.

The process of urbanisation in the Third World is creating enormous cities which have, as a consequence, enormous problems. In 1950 there were 1 billion people living in urban areas. By 1990 there were nearly 2.5 billion people living in urban areas. By the year 2000 there will be 3.2 billion urban dwellers. *Written in 1996 in 75/25*

By the year 2025, six out of ten children in the developing world will live in cities, and more than half of them will be poor. Urban children are at risk because cities are not conducive to their health and development.

Of the urban population of Bangladesh, 60.86 per cent lives below the poverty line. The figure for Dhaka city is 54 per cent, which probably indicates that there are more job opportunities in the big city.

Resource 3
Trafficking in women and children

In our story, Rosina was kidnapped on the street and would have been smuggled into India to be sold, to live like a slave, to make money for evil people. She escaped, but thousands do not; they live and die in misery.

Report in
The Bangladesh Observer
(one of the country's daily newspapers)

Trafficking in children should stop

100 children are smuggled out of the country each month and sent to the Middle East.

Children and women will be sacrificed at the altar of greed of a demon in the shape of a human.

The trafficking baron (believed to be a member of the Government) is too powerful to be touched. *31 October 2000*

Fact file

Bangladesh is the worst-affected country because
- it has a long and easily crossed border with India, making smuggling easy;
- so many people are poor it is easy to fool them with a promise of money and secure jobs out of the country.

UNICEF reports (1999) that an average of 4500 women and children are annually trafficked across the border to India.

The other principal countries affected are Nepal, India, Sri Lanka and Pakistan.

Trafficking in women and children is a gross violation of the Universal Declaration of Human Rights, 1948. It has been declared a 'Human Rights Crisis'.

CATW (Bangladesh) stands for Coalition Against Trafficking in Women and it represents 50 women's organisations in the East who are concerned about this evil.

It is a global problem. Recent research (19 December 2001) by the BBC has revealed that children from Africa are trafficked into Britain, to act as slaves in private homes and for benefit fraud.

Report in
The Independent
(Bangladesh daily newspaper)

Bid to smuggle out 19 Tribal children

An attempt to traffic in 19 minor tribal children was foiled yesterday by the police.

Acting on a tip-off the police stopped a van and found the abducted children. Seven youths have been arrested.

Activity

The above short news report could be the stimulus for creative writing or a classroom role-play or drama. Alternatively, for *older students*, the following might be used.

A tale of blood

A trafficker confessed and told the following story. The trafficker was from the village of Satkhira, near the Indian border. He said that some girls were trafficked in four phases during August and September. All of them were aged between 20 and 25 and had been working in the garment factories of Dhaka. One young woman in the group of five, called Jahanara, overheard a conversation between the traffickers and learnt that she had fallen into the hands of women traffickers. At the time they had crossed the Indian border at the Bhojabhanga canal and were residing at the residence of an Indian trafficker. Jahanara said that she wanted to go home. She was tortured and raped in front of the group. The others were speechless at the sight of such torture. All of them are now trapped in different brothels throughout India.

The humiliating procedure used by the pimps to sell the women, including young girls, was documented by an undercover reporter of the Urdu daily newspaper *Jung*. The 'commodity' is paraded in front of the buyers, each and every physical attribute of the woman is appraised according to the buyers' needs, skills are assessed and the bargaining begins. Eventually the women are auctioned off into servitude, if not right away, after a number of similar demeaning and degrading displays.

By Muid Khan Mamun
President of Human Rights Watch, Bangladesh

Violence against women in the Churches
(*taken from the leaflet 'Violence Against Women' published by Churches Together in England*)

Some survivors of abuse have experienced their local church as a safe and supportive place. However, evidence from across Europe reveals that significant numbers of men in positions of pastoral authority exploit the trust and confidence of their Church members by engaging in inappropriate sexual behaviour. This can happen in the context of counselling, confession, working relationships, youthwork, etc. Such behaviour is a result of:

• The abuse of power and authority;
• The lack of mutuality and equality;
• The absence of meaningful and informed consent.

Too many women, having expected help from the Church, have discovered that the priority is to protect the individual perpetrator and the reputation of the institution.

49

Contacts

Minister and Clergy Sexual Abuse Survivors (MACSAS)
c/o CSSA, BM-CSSA
London WC1N 3XX

The Women's Co-ordinating Group of Churches Together in England
CTE,
27 Tavistock Square
London WC1H 9HH

Trafficking in women
(taken from the leaflet 'Violence Against Women' published by Churches Together in England)

Trafficking of women and children into enforced prostitution is a virulent form of organised crime. Victims are subjected to false promises, intimidation, and acts of brutality. They are deprived of their human rights. Escaping from a gang of traffickers is almost impossible. Trafficking is a modern form of slavery. A recent consultation organised by the Conference of European Churches (CEC) highlighted the issues.

- A recent estimate suggests that hundreds of women are smuggled from Eastern Europe into the UK *each month* to work as prostitutes.
- NGO and police sources believe that over 100,000 women and girls from Eastern Europe have, in effect, been sold into slavery.

Contact

Global Alliance Against Traffic in Women
Website: http://www.inet.co.th/org/gaatw
CEC, PO Box 2100, 1505 Route de Ferney, Geneva 2

Resource 4
Street and abandoned children

Shahidha and Kwame are street children. There are many thousands of children who are without family love and support on the streets of all the cities of the developing world, whether they are in Africa, South America or Asia. These are the street children.

Children's rights

Ninety-nine per cent of the world's children now live in countries whose governments have committed themselves to the United Nations Convention on the Rights of the Child. Over 185 countries have ratified the Convention and aspire to give children a better future. It is now universally acknowledged that children's lives should be ones 'of joy and peace, of playing and learning and growing, their future shaped in harmony and co-operation.'
Anne Leahy, 75/25

The Ten Basic Rights of the Child

- Equality for every race, religion and nationality.
- Protection so as to develop fully.
- Name and nationality.
- Food, housing and medical care.
- Special care for the disabled/handicapped.
- Affection, love and understanding.
- Free education and play.
- The first to get help in an emergency.
- Protection from neglect, cruelty and exploitation.
- To grow in peace, tolerance and friendship.

However

Every week 250,000 children die as victims of malnutrition and illness.

An estimated 10 million children (in the year 2001), are infected by AIDS.

The total number of children in child labour exceeds 100 million.

Fifty per cent of the population of the many refugee camps around the world are children.

And the list goes on . . .

51

Street children

'Let the Children Live'

The funeral is the second of the week; the second of a young teenager. Probably a member of the *bandas*, or gangs engaged in a protection racket or a group of drug pushers, that dominate life in the *barrios* of Medellin. There will be another two funerals of young men or teenagers next week. Medellin is a city of easy money; and easy death. Last year there were 4,296 murders in the city – that's 11.75 murders a day! Families disintegrate; the children drift onto the streets. They live in the gutters among the rubbish and the rotting vegetables in the market. They become *gamines* (guttersnipes). Within days, these children, as young as six, are themselves on drugs; sniffing glue is the start. The children form gangs to protect one another. A gang will buy some DIY glue and share it among themselves. They squabble over it. It leads to fights, but it eases their pain, the hunger, the loneliness. They eat by pilfering, shoplifting, mugging. These children are no angels; they are filthy, dirty and foul-mouthed and aggressive. Shopkeepers and city 'worthies' want them 'disposed' of. Vigilantes hunt them and call them 'los desechables' – 'the disposable ones'.

Into this scene, in 1982, came Peter Walker, a young English student for the Anglican ministry. He was on holiday, exploring Colombia on the cheap. Failing to book a return flight, he was stranded for two weeks with all his money gone. He ended up sleeping rough and eating every second day. It was then that the *gamines* came to the rescue. They showed him the ropes; how to survive on the streets, where the safe places to sleep were, where to get cheap food. They even shared what little they had. When one of the street children collapsed at his feet, Peter carried him to the hospital. Peter could not believe that such things could happen in a Christian country. Boldly he went straight to the archbishop's palace and demanded to see the archbishop. Peter learnt of work already taking place and how caring the archbishop really was. He put a life-changing challenge to Peter: 'Perhaps God is asking you to do something for the street children.' Peter could not get the archbishop's words out of his head.

Returning to Britain, Peter raised money to return again, and again. Impressed with what the Catholic Church was attempting to do in Colombia, he became a Catholic and in 1995 was ordained to the priesthood, for the diocese of Medellin. He founded the charity 'Let the Children Live' and spends all his time working with and for the street children.

Father Peter Walker visits the UK two or three times a year and is very willing to accept an invitation to visit and speak at any school, primary or secondary. He is a very good speaker and uses very evocative visual material. Highly recommended, he can be contacted through: Ms Pauline Allan, 'Let the Children Live', Tel: 01302 858369.

Resource 5
Defence of tribal peoples

Fr Homerich, mentioned in the assembly, has lived among the tribal peoples of northern Bangladesh for 45 years. He has converted many to Christianity and been their champion and defender. As a minority group, the Mandi people are constantly oppressed by certain sections of the majority Bangli population.

Report in *Daily Star*

A group of Bengali settlers killed a young Garo mother in the Madhupur forest in the Tangail district on 20 March, leaving others in her tribe panic-stricken. Villagers said Gidita Rema, stabbed to death by 15 assailants, had been protesting the cruelties of the local Bangalees. It took place in the village where the Garo people grow pineapples and other seasonal fruits. The Bengali money lenders would often come and demand back the loans they often give without any proper agreements. Gidita's youngest brother also fell victim when he protested, however he managed to escape with his life. Police were informed but no effort was made to resolve the issue. A neighbour, anticipating more violence, said, 'We have been forced to obey the local Bangalees, they lay their hands on whatever we earn.'   *29 March 2001*

Fact file

A conference at the headquarters of the World Health Organisation in Geneva in January 2000 heard that indigenous people constitute 5 per cent of the world's population. Tribal people or indigenous people are found in 70 countries and are found in five or six thousand distinct ethnic groups. They have a great diversity of culture, language and heritage. The wide diversity of biological background is of vital importance to humanity.

Sadly, it was revealed, indigenous people have a life expectancy at birth that is 10 to 20 years less than the rest of the population around them. Malnutrition and communicable diseases, like yellow fever and TB, continue to affect a large proportion of the indigenous population.

Development ventures are also taking their toll. For example, on the Indonesian island of Kalimantan, since 1970 the degradation of the world's oldest rain forest is destroying the lives of the 3 million Dayak people. The WHO called for partnerships between governments and the indigenous people movement.

By Gro Halem Brundtland, Director General of WHO

Ownership and access to land is an issue of immense importance to tribal and indigenous people everywhere. Some indigenous land rights are customary ones, dating back to 'time immemorial', some were formalised under colonial rule. Other rights have been lost, disregarded by governments or ignored by the majority community, while tribal lands are often stolen by individual settlers, government agencies and by public and private companies. The Adivasi – the preferred generic name of the tribal peoples of Bangladesh – are today fighting to retain their already tenuous rights to land.

Minority Rights International Report, 1991

Resource 6
The role of women

Many hundreds of thousands of women in Bangladesh and other developing nations are working hard to improve the position and role of women in society, especially in Islamic countries. Thousands of women's groups have brought confidence, self-respect and a sense of dignity to women in many developing countries.

Lack of respect for women

Report in
Hotline Bangladesh

A 25-year-old housewife died on 28 September when her husband beat her, poured kerosene on her and set her on fire. Her dowry of 3000 taka (£40) was due that day. When his wife failed to bring it he took drastic action.

Another action against women is acid throwing. On 30 October a Bangladesh newspaper reported that 90 women had suffered acid being thrown in their faces.

This was usually done by jilted lovers and demanding husbands. *October 2000*

It's still a man's world

In politics, worldwide:
- 90 per cent of seats in parliaments are held by men;
- 10 per cent of seats are held by women;
- 94 per cent of national cabinets are occupied by men;
- 6 per cent are occupied by women.

Earned income, worldwide:
- 74 per cent men's share
- 26 per cent women's share *(1995 figures)*

Fact file

- Out of 1.3 billion people living in absolute poverty over 70 per cent are women.
- At the present rate of progress it will take another 475 years before women reach equality with men as managers in the workplace. (Presently only 10 per cent are women, but they make up half of the world's workforce.)
- One in three households is headed by women (the men have been killed by local war, AIDS or have migrated).
  Result of a survey of 75 developing nations
- Female-headed families are the poorest in the world.
- 64 per cent of the world's illiterates are women.
- In the year 2000 half of the world's workforce were women.

- An African woman's risk of dying from pregnancy and at childbirth is 1 in 23 compared to 1 in 4000 in wealthy countries.
- At least 2 million girls between 4 and 8 undergo genital mutilation each year.

'Before it was a silent life'

Before it was a silent life between men and women. They never spoke to one another, not even husband and wife. Neighbouring women would pass the evenings chatting and spinning, and you would talk to other women at the wells or the grinding stone. Women never spoke in the presence of men: they'd be ashamed and above all scared that they would be beaten. So women kept their ideas to themselves, even if these would have been a help to the community. Women are never allowed to inherit the land of their husband. As this is normal here, women did not complain, thinking that's how things are.

62-year-old Fatimata from Burkina Faso

She concludes: 'We now have women who preside over meetings in the village. Development projects have helped women greatly.'

Resource 7
Safe water and sanitation

Fact file

- 4.4 billion people live in the developing countries.
- Three-fifths lack basic sanitation.
- Almost one-third have no access to clean water.
- 10 million children under five die each year (most due to lack of a safe water supply).
- Only 34 per cent of people on planet Earth have access to adequate sanitation, i.e. clean water and sewage systems.

Using ICT

Try these websites

www.who.int/whosis	World Health Organisation
www.jrf.org.uk	Joseph Rowntree Foundation

An example of action due to aid provided by CAFOD

(This story can be dramatised in the classroom.)

In Kuru, in Nigeria, the streams were contaminated by salmonella, worms and E-coli bacteria, and the people regularly suffered from severe stomach pains and diarrhoea. The danger to children was the worst of all. For them, these terrible diseases could be fatal.

CAFOD provided the money and its local partner helped the local people to build a water filter in their village. The villagers provided the sand, gravel and charcoal and did all the work ... then the wonderful moment came when the first bucket of water was poured through the filter. It went in, dark green and foul-smelling, and just ten minutes later, clean, pure water poured out from the bottom. 'No more worries,' declared the village chief.

Now, to the people of Kuru, constant disease and sickness is a thing of the past.

Question: Who, in this class, would be prepared to drink from the first bucket of water? If you would not be prepared to do that, realise what the alternative is – drinking the original 'dark green, foul-smelling water'.

Resource 8
Relief work

Puspa and her family lost their home due to unexpected flooding coming from a late monsoon storm in the Himalayas. All disasters are sudden and often with little or no warning.

Fact file

- Bangladesh is at risk from cyclones and floods every six years.
- In 1991, 140,000 people were killed by the strong winds and tidal waves of 7 m. The homeless were numbered at 1.7 million.
- About 95 per cent of deaths caused by disasters occur in poor countries.
- In richer countries the costs of rebuilding after a disaster are high, but there is always more money and more technology for reconstruction.
- The uncontrolled spread of infectious diseases such as AIDS, diarrhoea and malaria takes more lives than disasters.

Activity

Imagine

Imagine that you are a poor farmer living in Bangladesh. You have, with your own hands, rebuilt your mud house; but you know that, after a while, the cyclones will return.

Discuss

What will you do to protect your family? What help and resources do you need? What should the government do?

Reveal

In 1997 a worse cyclone than the one that hit Bangladesh in 1991, struck the country. Winds of 150 miles per hour blew for ten hours. As a result, half a million people lost their homes. How many people died this time? Answer: only 100 people lost their lives. That is because 142 concrete cyclone shelters had been built (12 were paid for by CAFOD, England). People had also been trained to warn others when there were signs of an approaching cyclone.

In normal times each concrete shelter, standing on huge concrete legs, or supports, is used as a school for the local children.

Use of ICT

Try the following websites for more information

www.disasterrelief.org American Red Cross

www.redcross.org.uk British Red Cross

www.foe.org.uk Friends of the Earth

www.greenpeace.org Greenpeace

www.unep.org United Nations Environment Programme

What is?

What is a disaster? A disaster is often sudden. It causes great damage, destruction and human suffering.

Try this

Hold a class debate on:

'It is more important to reduce poverty around the world than to raise money for disaster relief.'

Deadly disasters 1990–2000

Year	Location	Death Toll	Disaster
1990	Iran	36,000	earthquake
1991	Bangladesh	140,000	cyclone
1995	Japan	6300	earthquake
1996	China	531	landslide
1997	Montserrat	32	volcano
1998	Central America	10,000	hurricane
1999	Turkey	16,000	earthquake
2000	Mozambique	650	floods

Class discussion

Which type of disaster do you think is the worst? Which of the above countries recovered the most quickly from their disaster? (Answer: the richest. Why do the rich recover more quickly? How can people protect themselves against such disasters?)

Resource 9
Caste – Untouchables

The Hindu people living in Bangladesh, near the border with India, are, in the main, of the caste called the untouchables. This is the lowest caste, which is not considered fit to mix with the other Hindu castes. Naturally, Christians, with Christ's love of the poor before them, make a special effort to serve and provide for the untouchables.

In Indian society (Bangladesh was once considered part of India) two terms have caused confusion: 'class' and 'caste'. There are four classes – the Brahmin priests; the Kshatria, ruler-warriors; the Vaishya, merchants and farmers; and the Shudra, the servants. When the Portuguese arrived in India in the sixteenth century, they applied the word 'casta' to any tribal or family group. There are many more castes than classes. 'Out-castes' were beyond the whole system. Mahatma Gandhi tried to elevate the outcasts, or untouchables, as they were also called. He sought to raise the lot of the untouchables by calling them 'Harijans' ('God's people'), leading them into forbidden temples and getting them the vote.

Among the tribals, particularly the Paharias people of northwest Bangladesh, the family of a deceased person is considered 'unclean' and untouchable.

> The family members of the deceased are considered untouchables. For example, outsiders will not accept anything from their hands; they must keep some distance from others and they cannot share the communal water pipe with others.

This 'unclean' situation is only lifted after the *sradha*, which is a feast that can take place any time from ten days to a year after the death of the loved one. It is an important feast given in honour of the dead relative and only after it is the veil of pollution on the family lifted.

Resource 10
Education for the poor

Shahidha, in our story, could only get to school of an evening because she had to work during the day to help support her family. This is true of countless children in the developing nations. If they do not work they will have nothing to eat; education comes second to simply starving.

Interviewing a working child about education

Julekha is now 11 years of age. She was working in a garment factory before starting at a BRAC school in Rampura. At the factory she earned 500 taka (£6.50) a month. She was totally illiterate before but is now in class 2. 'I was illiterate before but now I can read and write so many things. I want to learn more. It's very enjoyable at school, better than the tough life in the garment factory.' Julekha still works part-time as a maid, but her new employers encourage her to attend school in the afternoons and the evening.

UCEP stands for Underprivileged Children's Educational Programmes, Bangladesh. It addresses its services to the most poor and distressed children in large city areas. These poor working and street children, one of the most vulnerable of all groups, are forced into the workforce by the extreme poverty of their families. UCEP provides:

1. Basic education
2. Vocational/technical training
3. Job placement.

The children who attend a UCEP school continue to work and earn. The schools operate a three-shift day, each shift giving only three lessons for a class. A child can attend during a shift convenient to him/her. The teachers are specially trained also to provide social work and support.

Resource 11
Interfaith relations

Ahmed was willing to pray with and for Christians. There are many people in Asian countries working for better relations between the different world religions. In Bangladesh, for example, an outstanding example is Sister Eugenia, who spends much of her time working to improve relationships between the different Christian communities in Bangladesh and the majority Islamic faith.

Fact file

The Government of Bangladesh, respecting the Christian faith, has declared Christmas Day a national holiday (1993). That year the President and the Prime Minister, in their separate Christmas messages, wished Christians a merry Christmas and sought the support of the Christian community in building the nation.

The Catholic Commission for Justice and Peace (GPO Box 5, Dhaka–1000) in October 2001, issued a summary of seven excerpts from seven different newspapers. Each one accuses Christian agencies (with no evidence or proof provided) of bringing money into the country to convert people to Christianity. One even goes so far as to claim that an aid agency was training troops. As the Commission points out, there is no evidence to support these wild assertions. They do, however, reflect the widespread fear and anxiety about the motives of Christians.

Newspaper report

The Catholic Church in Bangladesh under the leadership of the local bishops and sometimes jointly with other Churches, has been carrying out inter-religious dialogue with a three-fold aim: (a) To awaken interest among the Christians in the inter-religious dialogue; (b) to help Christians to know and better understand and respect the followers of Islam and (c) to foster good relations, co-operation and harmony with them and their communities. The following areas may be underlined: *Dialogue of Life* – where Muslims and Christians live and work together. By personal contacts, visits, friendships; attending one another's naming ceremonies, weddings, etc. *Dialogue of Action* – The Church takes Muslim brothers and sisters as co-operators in educational and health schemes. *Dialogue of Discourse* – In some common gatherings of Christians and Muslims, religious leaders are invited to share their own faith-reflection on issues like injustices, poverty, social and moral evils, etc. *Dialogue of Spirituality* – Some efforts are being made to give spiritual formation, by readings from the Holy Books, songs and prayers, etc.

By Bishop Patrick D'Rozario, 22 October 1998

From the Koran

The Koran calls Christians the 'nearest in love' to the Muslims, whom it instructs to 'dispute not with the People of the Book' – that is, Christians and Jews – 'save in the most courteous manner . . . and say, "We believe in what has been sent down to us and what has been sent down to you; our God and your God is one".'

Quoted in The Tablet, *22 December 2001*

The Koran diverges from the basic narrative of the gospels – such as the very full but oddly unfamiliar description it gives of the first Christmas. In this Koranic version, Jesus' birth takes place not in a stable but under a palm tree in an oasis. Shortly afterwards the Christ child, still in swaddling clothes, sits up and addresses Mary's family with the words, 'I am the servant of the God. He has given me the Gospel and ordained me a prophet.'

Quoted in The Tablet, *22 December 2001*

Resource 12
Fair trading – the garment workers

Ashma and millions of other children and young people have to earn money to live on in the factories that make our clothes.

Fact file

- When you buy a pair of trainers that cost £44, only £1.71 goes to the workers in Asia who made them.
- Transnational corporations (TNCs) account for two-thirds of world trade. These corporations include Unilever (brands like Flora, Bird's Eye, Brooke Bond), Nestlé (Nescafé, Quality Street, Crosse and Blackwell), Shell. These TNCs control two-thirds of the world's trade. They earn and manage more money than most countries do.
- The global textile trade is worth 350 billion US dollars.

Activity

Write to Fairtrade at Suite 204, 16 Baldwin's Gardens, London, EC1N 7RJ and send a donation of £5. For this you will receive a pack containing a video about fair trading of bananas, a game and lots of samples of chocolate, tea, coffee, etc. Use on a small stall to get orders to support Fairtrade.

Use of ICT

Try the following for more information

www.cafod.org.uk

www.sciaf.org.uk

www.christian-aid.org.uk

www.wto.org

www.fairtrade.org.uk

www.anitaroddick.com

News reports:
Daily Star

It is becoming like a nightmare for Bangladesh's readymade garments (RMG) sector, as the developing and least developed countries are positioning themselves in the global trade arena through different bilateral and multilateral trade agreements. Bangladesh is finding that it is losing out to countries like Nigeria, Honduras and China.

In recent months a number of major buyers have already withdrawn from Bangladesh, finding cheaper options elsewhere. *23 October 2001*

Daily Star

Fire at garments factory kills 12

Twelve people, ten of them female, died of suffocation when a fire broke out in the Banani area of Dhaka city in the early hours of yesterday. The incident took place after 150 workers of Globe Knitting Ltd, went to sleep at 2.30am under their sewing machines.

The factory, which is housed on the fourth and sixth floors of a seven-floor building, has no emergency exit. The workers were asleep at 3.30am when they were awakened by thick smoke. Workers said that the main entrance of each floor was locked. The supervisor, who had the keys, claims that he unlocked the entrances when he heard the cries of the trapped workers. Ten fire units attended the fire and 50 workers were rescued by the firefighters. According to witnesses and police most of the trapped workers escaped by breaking down a wall. *28 August 2000*

Star Report (*same issue of the newspaper*)

At least 100 workers have been killed and several hundred others injured in fire-related incidents in garment factories in the last few years.

Daily Star

50 hurt as fire exit collapses

At least 50 workers were injured when they scrambled for safety following a fire alarm at a garments factory in Tejgaon region of Dhaka, yesterday. The incident occurred at 6.30pm when a machine caught fire. Workers were injured when the overloaded fire exit ladder of the multistorey factory collapsed. This incident follows the one in August when 12 workers died. *30 October 2000*

Daily Star

Death Toll 48: Most killed in stampede

The death toll at the Chowdhury Knitwear Factory rose to 48, with over 100 injured. Investigators have discovered that a security guard had locked a gate causing the death of the 48 garment workers. Only four died in the fire itself, the rest died from suffocation and in the stampede. The fire originated from a spark in a machine used for erasing stains from cloth. Alam, a 12-year-old worker, wrongly pushed the machine's plug into a socket causing the spark. Though most workers managed to escape the building 250 women and children on the fourth floor stampeded to get down the narrow staircase. Then they discovered they had been locked in. Firefighters and local people eventually broke open the gate. The managing director, Sagor Chowdhury, denied the allegation that the gate was locked. *27 November 2000*

Daily Star

A living hell

Further enquiries at the Chowdhury Knitwear Factory in the Narsingdi District, following the disastrous fire of 26 November 2000, when 48 workers died, have revealed a living hell. Witnesses have confirmed that the security guard, Abdul Jalil, acting on instructions from the management, locked the exit door, preventing the escape of the workers. Zakir Hossain (30) told that the workers are subjected to inhuman conditions. In spite of factory regulations, employees are forced to work 14 hours each day, from 8am until 10pm, and very often are made to work 20 hours a day. And each worker only gets 500 taka a month [equivalent to £7]. Moreover they are not paid regularly, sometimes the salary is given on 25th of the next month, and so no worker can leave the job.

Abdus Samad (27) said that on the day of the fire everyone was trapped and he escaped by breaking a window and climbing down a pipe. He was severely burnt but cannot afford any medication since he has not been paid for two months.

A number of female workers, who wished to remain anonymous, informed the investigators that they were frequently subjected to oppression, deprivation and harassment.

Aziza (22) from the sewing section said that apart from the 14 hours of working, they had to work late at night. They only received one piece of bread and a banana to sustain them, until they were released from work at 2 or 3 in the morning.

An initial investigation revealed that at least 400 of the 900 workers at the factory were children. On being questioned the General Manager stated that there were no child workers at his factory. When he was shown the names and ages of the dead children from the fire he did not make any comment! The courts have ordered the Chowdhury company to pay compensation to the families of those who have died.

It is not only the owner and employer, and others in the factory administration, who have the deaths of so many on their heads. It is also the corruption in the government administration, especially the Factories Inspectors, who are contributing to the inhumane working conditions and the untimely deaths of so many

Odhikar, 24 December 2000

They say, what do they say?

I won't shop at Asda. Why? Because since 1999, it has been owned by the American giant Wal-Mart, a company that, to me, represents everything that is bad about the globalising impulses of big business.

I think of the ongoing search for ever-cheaper labour as a race to the bottom. But it's Wal-Mart which comes out on top. Their annual sales of $137.6 billion are larger than the Gross Domestic Product of 155 countries in the world (and there are only 192). And these sales are generated from the labour of people such as the workers of China who are trapped in 10-hour shifts, seven days a week for 12 cents an hour.

Wal-Mart uses tens of thousands of similar factories around the world.

Anita Roddick in The Big Issue, *22 October 2001*

Resource 13
Training schemes

Dullchander learnt his potter's skills from his father; but there is no future for his son. He needs to benefit from modern engineering training. Education and training for a skilled job are the passport out of poverty.

Note: See also resource 10 on page 62

Basic education for all is still not the rule in Bangladesh. While most children are enrolled for primary education, only 50 per cent attend regularly and 65 per cent drop out before the end of primary education. Fewer girls complete primary education. Thus the formal education system is considered quite wasteful and unproductive. The nonformal basis of education gains in importance. Essentially it is an out-of-school response to people's needs to develop their potential. Children from poor families are able to work and to learn. The UCEP (Underprivileged Children's Education Programme) addresses its services to the most poor and distressed children in large city areas. It strives to

- provide a basic education;
- provide vocational/technical training;
- provide job placement and employment support.

Employable Skills Training

UCEP designs its skills training to suit the market needs of skilled and semi-skilled labour. Thus the training is adapted to the modules of employable skills. This is done in close consultation, primarily with the industrial employers.

Dr Ahmadullah Mia

An example

Rehana (16) is studying at the Women's Literacy Centre, Chittagong. Her father is an office cleaner and could not dream of having enough money to send his daughter to school. Rehana learns Bengali from 3pm to 4.30pm each day after finishing her daily work as a cleaner. Besides Bengali, she can learn basic health, hygiene and sanitation education, and a little English. 'I am very happy to learn,' Rehana says, 'because I always wanted to read the street signs and the posters.'

At a nearby school run by UCEP the instructor said, 'We don't ask for any sophisticated equipment, but we want enough money to supply the children with a slate each. These will be easier to write on, because notebooks are usually not hard enough to use as the children sit on the ground.'

Resource 14
Human rights

Rosalind bravely makes known, through her newsletter and internet contacts, the evil actions of some people in Bangladesh society. Prompted by her love of her country and her deep Christian faith, Rosalind fearlessly reports things that are wrong, like injustices by the police and corruption among politicians.

Declarations

United Nations Covenant on Civil and Political Rights 1966

In those States in which ethnic, religious or linguistic minorities exist, persons belonging to such minorities shall not be denied the right, in community with the other members of their group, to enjoy their own culture, to profess and practise their own religion, or to use their own language.

Universal Islamic Declaration of Human Rights 1981

The rights of minorities

The Qur'anic principle, 'There is no compulsion in religion' shall govern the religious rights of non-Muslim minorities.

In a Muslim country, religious minorities shall have the choice to be governed in respect of their civil and personal matters by Islamic law, or by their own laws.

Amnesty International

When the first two hundred letters came, the guards gave me back my clothes. Then the next two hundred came and the prison director got in touch with his superior. The letters kept coming and coming; they still kept coming and the President called the prison and told them to let me go. The President called me to his office and said to me, 'How is it that a trade union leader, like you, has so many friends all over the world?' He showed me an enormous box full of letters he had received and when we parted, he gave them to me. I still have them.

This is how one Dominican Republic trade unionist described the results of the work of one of the world's most popular and effective human rights organisations, Amnesty International.

One of Amnesty's most effective methods of putting pressure on governments to release prisoners of conscience (those detained for their beliefs, colour, sex, ethnic origin, religion) is through encouraging its members to send letters of protest to prison authorities, Ministries of Justice, Presidents, etc.)

Amnesty also campaigns against the death penalty and torture. It has more than 750,000 members in over 150 countries and 3800 local groups in Africa, the Americas, Europe and the Middle East.

The symbol of Amnesty is the lighted candle, which, according to the founder Peter Benenson, 'burns not for us, but for all those who we failed to rescue from prison, who were shot on the way to prison, who were tortured, who were kidnapped, who "disappeared".'

Twin Towers – twin terrors

There were two 'Reigns of Terror', if we could but remember and consider it; the one wrought murder in hot passions, the other in heartless cold blood; the one lasted mere months, the other had lasted a thousand years; the one inflicted death upon a thousand persons, the other upon a hundred million; but our shudders are all for the 'horrors' of the . . . momentary Terror, so to speak; whereas, what is the horror of swift death by the axe compared with lifelong death from hunger, cold, insult, cruelty and heartbreak? A city cemetery could contain the coffins filled by that brief Terror, which we have all been so diligently taught to shiver at and mourn over; but all France could hardly contain the coffins filled by that older and real Terror – that unspeakable bitter and awful Terror which none of us has been taught to see in its vastness or pity as it deserves.

Mark Twain, writing about the French Revolution in A Connecticut Yankee in King Arthur's Court. *Quoted in* New Internationalist *of November 2001*

On the day of the unspeakable terrorist outrage on 11 September 2001

- 24,000 people died of hunger;
- 6020 children died of diarrhoea;
- 2700 children died of measles.

- Number of malnourished children in developing countries, 149 million;
- Number of people without access to safe drinking water, 1100 million;
- Number of people without access to adequate sanitation, 2400 million;
- Number of people living on less than one dollar a day, 1200 million;
- Number of African children under 15 living with HIV, 1.1 million.

Resource 15
Self-respect

Rich or poor, every human person can have dignity and respect for him- or herself; and should be accorded it by others. Indeed many in the wealthy northern nations have every material possession and comfort, but lack self-respect.

News story
Daily Star

Jesmin's dream never came true

Jesmin's recent dream was to build a tin-shed house in her village at Burirchar in Pirojpur district. The 15-year-old girl's dream never came true. She was killed in the stampede at her workplace, Shanghai Apparel Ltd, in the city [of Dhaka] on 30 July.

Jesmin, the eldest of five sisters and a brother, came to Dhaka two years ago to escape from poverty. She discontinued her studies after class five. In Dhaka she shared a nine feet by eight feet makeshift room with her aunt and uncle. 'She slept on the earthen floor of the room so that she did not have to share the 300 taka rent of the place' said her uncle. 'Jesmin told us all yesterday that she did not want to go to work. But the owners had warned the day before that if any worker was missing for half the day, she would be considered absent for three days,' said Jesmin's auntie, adding that Jesmin was afraid of losing her wages. 'She calculated her working days carefully and dreamt of building a tin-shed house in Burichar. She would reject marriage proposals for this reason,' said her grandmother. Liton, Jesmin's cousin, described how they had gone to work together as usual. At about 2pm, when the fire broke out, the lights failed and the panic seized the workers. 'I looked for her, but she was not there. I scrambled to the roof and jumped to the roof of another building two stories lower down. I was badly hurt.' Jesmin died in the stampede down the narrow exit stairs. (23 other female garment workers died in that fire.)   *3 August 1997*

Hands

Reflective observations in Bangladesh

The cupped hands of the beggar woman

The strong, sensitive, hands of the potter

The open hands of the untouchables

The joined hands in greeting and salute

The smooth hands of the young female teacher

The calloused hands of the rickshaw puller
The gnarled hands of the ferry oarsman
The guiding hands of the ploughing farmer
The nibbled hands of the garment worker
The eager hands of the shoeshine boy
The greasy hands of the market trader
The bound, shaking, hands of the abducted child
The rough, swift hands of the weaver
The languid hands of the traffic cop.
You meet the poor when you observe their hands.

Resource 16
Working together – microcredit groups

'Working together we achieve more' is a phrase often used in schools. It is obviously true and eminently applicable to the struggles of the populations of the developing nations, as they use micro-credit groups to cast off poverty.

Quote

Microcredit was invented by poor women as a strategy for survival.
Bangladesh Observer

Fact file

Microcredit groups began about 50 years ago.
Professor Yunus of Bangladesh gave the groups the institutional shape as tools of development which they have today.

Quote

Never doubt that a small group of committed citizens can change the world. Indeed, it is the only thing that ever has.
Margaret Mead

Grameen Bank

The world-famous Grameen Bank began in the village of Jobra in Bangladesh in response to the needs of the poor woman (and the hundreds of thousands like her) described below.

Today the Grameen Bank employs a staff of over 14,000 and works in 35,000 of Bangladesh's estimated 68,000 villages. It lends out over half a billion dollars each year; it has an education programme that reaches over 12 million of the world's poorest. Its clientele is 94 per cent women. Its loan repayment rate is 98 per cent and has encouraged local savings to a total well over $96 million and has succeeded in taking countless hundreds of thousands of the poor out of poverty.

Banking by and for the poor

I learned so many things, I started thinking this is the real university I missed out all my life . . . one woman's story led me to a series of events which finally culminated into a very special kind of bank. I came across a woman who earned only two pennies a day by making bamboo stools. I couldn't accept why anybody should work so hard and make only two pennies. She explained why she makes two pennies. She doesn't have the money to buy the bamboo which goes into the bamboo stool. So she had to borrow the money from the trader, the trader who buys the final product. He lends her the money to buy the bamboo. When he buys the final product, he offers her a price which barely covers the cost of the raw materials. Her labour comes almost free, she works almost like a slave. I said to myself, there is no reason why it should be this way. This can be solved easily. It doesn't need big theories to solve this.

Professor Mohammud Yunus, founder of the Grameen Bank